Coffee and Papercuts

Poetry and Prose

By
Leah Bailey

Conscious Dreams
P U B L I S H I N G

Coffee and Papercuts: Poetry and Prose

Copyright © 2022: Leah Bailey

First Printed in United Kingdom 2022

Published by Conscious Dreams Publishing

Edited by Elise Abram

Typeset by Oksana Kosovan

www.consciousdreamspublishing.com

@consciousdreamspublishing

ISBN: 978-1-915522-00-9

Dedication

For all the souls who have, at some point,
suffered from imposter syndrome.

Contents

Poetry

Various types and styles
brewed fresh

Many, many, gates
between here and the car.
I was so little.

Goldfinch

Through my window while I work,
one flits to my front yard . . .
Beautiful,
colourful, curious
and disappears.
This saddens me.

It returns,
it brings a friend.
Now, I'm trying to focus
on my screen
where I want
my conversation
to flow . . .
Difficult enough
over the laptop
without me
distracted
by wings and flits
of colour
out of my window.

What a gift.
To see this
sitting still,
as I wouldn't be . . .
any
other
time.

Mother Nature Mocks

The irony of snow on the weekend,
when you're little and hoping
for the day off school . . .

The irony of a rainstorm,
when there is a picnic
and you forgot your umbrella . . .

The irony of gorgeous sunshine,
when work or health
keeps you inside looking out . . .

The best laid plans,
laid to waste in irony
when Mother Nature mocks.

Like a Love Song

The music moves me, out of my reverie.
Though I can hope and dream and sing along...
life tells me that kind of love's not meant to be.
Searching for a soulmate like all the love songs.

Someone who sees all of me, through and through...
nothing but youthful fairy tales of my dreams.
Wanting, needing, a thing doesn't make it true.
All of them, loving all of me... not as it seems.

Thinking out loud of a love that will last
for all my life... strong and steady throughout?
Can't be sure of a future that treasures a broken past.
Promises to love, young or old, come to doubt.

Forget the world to chase cars, before we're old?
Fades into a highway horizon, the ache moves on.
At times love is buried beneath the lies we're told;
giving all, heart and soul, doesn't mean we've won.

Letting go of hope for "just the way you are",
I try to lessen my need to not end alone.
If I must... abandon all my deserved care,
to hold its shadow, before what's left is gone.

Amazed, I believe, when you do what you do,
that I might spend all my life, with love out of reach.
Whispering at night, "just one more dream that's true."
Where my heart races, e'en I run out of speech.

No sculptor or potions could ever sway me,
listening for your song, forever twinned with mine.
Something longs for how wonderful life would be,
loving someone like a love song I'd give my all to find.

For Caleb

– 13 –

Uncomfortable Conversations

When you don't know what to say.
When, "I'm sorry" or "I wish I could help"
isn't enough by a long . . . long way.
You understand, you empathise, it's felt . . .
but you're lost as to what you can do
and wish the task wasn't up to you.

A friend's ex making them suffer pain,
biting your lip instead of blooding theirs.
How can they, after love, bring such rain,
pour salt to enflame the smallest cares?
How can a reversal of all that once was
make demon of beloved with almost no cause?

Watch someone, so used to being put last,
believe it's their fault, sets me in a rage.
We all deserve decency no matter our past.
Our wants have value, don't accept the cage.
You matter, stand up and say what you need!
Narcissists otherwise hunger and feed.

The "guest" creates silence on the outside
in family warzones, that never say end.
Smiling civility, the drama it's best to hide;
the appearance of serenity in front of the friend.
Temporary reprieve, to create holiday peace . . .
until war, lost with time, makes light trouble cease.

"Your child is failing." no parent wants to hear.
Not their fault, it's just what is with books.
Other skills (also valuable) even if parents fear
they're less stable or respected might bring looks.
Value should be equal, work on cars or in courts . . .
learning's unequal but should not be found short.

Your aunt is passing, nothing to be done . . .
the third and fourth . . . wish though you might . . .
no change but comfort, no effort, no battle to be won.
All the loving will in the world can't always fight,
generations pass both behind and ahead of us.
Their legacy is ours, their memory, immortality, our trust.
They make room for who follows, as we all must.

Uncomfortable conversations move us all forward in time.
They're not meant to be comfortable, life is the mouth
of all our discomfort; theirs, yours, most especially mine.
It evolves us, moves us, inches closer to the truth.
We are always more than we think we can be;
takes less than we think to make us all more free.

When

When the heat finally breaks,
when the rains come
that sapped strength
returns, but only some.
When you get that first smile,
when you feel you're seen,
that lost soul, heart,
wonders where you've been.
When the music makes you pulse,
when life rushes through
the joy can return
it's all up to you . . .

When the heat finally broke,
and the rains finally came,
my heart trembling spoke,
my soul cautiously tame.
A breath was all it took,
between heat and the first drop.
So casually shoulder shook,
Now rain may never stop.

Both Weal and Warning

They say...
The only certain things
in life: death and taxes.
In which some truth may ring.

I say...
One more idea persists,
eternal change for all,
the kind no one resists.

We say...
"Why'd it happen to me?"
Better question to ask,
"What other way could be?"

You say...
"Seems like pain never ends!"
But dark contrasts the light,
counting blessings life sends.

Life says...
"This, too, shall pass away."
Truth in good times and bad.
N'er wiser warning say.

Variant Blue

In the night; from the depths; downcast and despondent;
the brackish mire of a melancholy mood . . .
causes us to reach high and shift, sift in the wind,
searching the change of shade, cool, calm and sparkling.

Rain and rapture wash clean a sapphire in the rough;
when seas rock us in grim gloom and we gaze glumly.
Dismal, darkness . . . indigo invading our eyes . . .
disconsolate, dejected hearts with navy night.

From ocean to sky and back our spirits slip in . . .
azure dreams bring a cobalt cloudless canopy.
Summer springs a heaven of the royal blue bells,
blushing beryl when wisps of iris wink and wave.

Forget-me-nots tell us not to neglect music,
songs sung with a full heart and a troubled spirit,
the blues in all variations, search for freedom,
one note, one petal, one drop, one breath at a time.

Humbling size
diving beneath my feet,
below the surface.

Bloody Mary Kind of Day

Today is not a day for wine,
not quite enough to do the job.
I'm sure later it will all be fine
but right now, my head throbs.
I know it's not as bad as it feels,
it's been so much worse before . . .
Mentally listing, the mind reels.
One or two, or three, maybe more.
Meeting with friendly faces to say,
"How are you, anything I can do?"
Me? It's a Bloody Mary kind of day,
thanks for being friends like you.

Photo by: @simbailey.photography

Good Fences

||||||||||||||||||||||||||||||||||||||||||||||||||||||||||

We create these walls around us
build them stone by stone
each betrayal fells, astounds us,
until we all end up alone.

||||||||||||||||||||||||||||||||||||||||||||||||||||

Sometimes they're weak, flimsy,
mesh or wood, with gates,
to be torn down with whimsy,
abandoned to their fates.

|||||||||||||||||||||||||||||||||||||||||||||||||

More often, fortress or cliffs
surround us on all sides.
Above the parapet never lifts
our hearts, hands, ears . . . eyes.

||||||||||||||||||||||||||||||||||||||||||||||||

Batterings we've felt before
make us hide in a solid shell.
Determined not to bear more,
Catapult or gentle knock who can tell?

|||||||||||||||||||||||||||||||||||||||||||||||

Make the mask, brick by brick,
Paint it bright to seem to invite,
Better and better fences, that's the trick,
Until crushing walls are all that seem right.

||||||||||||||||||||||||||||||||||||||||||||||||||||||||||

Lunacy

Gravity impacts the dance below,
shifting shades sink slowly,
lapping lazily at silver sands.
Blues and greys, the diaphanous cloth
dressed and trimmed in her best white foam.
Furious fighting, flurry and froths
when the love of the wind cuts in,
stealing the partner from the moon.
Increasing the depth, breadth and clefts
of waves till the waltz disappears
and the frenzy of a fevered furor
takes its place; lightning lit.
The bass and percussion of thunder
rolls reminiscent of the reeling
water wailing in the watch of
the displaced and desolate stars,
who can only watch and wait out the storm
for low tide and rest from
the lunacy and nature of the sea.

Cumulative Effect

There is a point we all must hide,
where our phone packed up and died,
where our laptop fritzed and cried,
where someone stole and cheated, lied.

There is a point where, "one more thing..."
is one too many, too far a bell to ring;
where the jangled edges crawl and sting;
idioms unbearably bad we fling.

Every direction deserved or not,
every inflection, every language we've got.
Anyone doesn't like it they can rot...
sail south where it's nice and hot.

There is only so much one mind can take;
when politeness is too hard to fake;
when everything inside you will just break;
if just one more hand we need to shake.

So, excuse me when I hit the deck.
Let me be sure, positive and check
the cumulative need to deflect...
or watch me turn into a nervous wreck.

"She was worth a stare. She was trouble."
Raymond Chandler — The Big Sleep

Noir

She was there, always is, there . . .
waiting in the shadows of the bar.
Half-lidded eyes, half-empty glass, hair
in golden waves, cascading, that are
perfect and ruffled just so . . .
Mysteriously alone, by choice maybe?
Without approaching, impossible to know.
But do you dare approach? Do you just see
a damsel in distress, femme fatale, a dame?
Men sweat and women scowl in her gaze,
the mystery allure that brings both fame
and ignominy, both in a Manhattan haze.
The tilt of her chin, her shoulders set,
defiant desperation for saving grace,
sullied innocence is what you get
with the noir woman's silk and lace.

Let Them Climb

To date, or not to date? That is the question.
Whether tis healthier in mind to endure the lines
and lameness of drunken meat market,
or to take online the sea of fake profiles
and by accepting end this.

To love — to dream — not alone, and by a kiss to say we end
the heartache and endless meals made for one
that loneliness is heir to: tis a consummation devoutly desired.

To date, to see,
to see, perchance to dream — ay, there's the flaw:
for in sight of that date . . . what dreams may come?

When we have shuffled off this mortal coil
this must give us hope — there is a love that makes
worthy time of so long a life . . .

For who would bear the heartbreak and scorns of time;
the cheater's lies; the narcissist's absence; the pangs of
lost love; the late man's excuses; the denial of responsibility;
and the rejection that deserving women receive . . .
when she herself might her peace make
with an ice cream tub?

Who would 'less than' bear,
to cry and worry under a 'less than' love,
but that the dread of marching alone until death
and the undiscovered country,
with no eternal heavenly love awaiting,
frightens us, and makes us rather bear the one we have
than fly to others, more worthy,
that we know not of?

Thus, cowardice makes slaves of us all, and
thus the self-worth of our soul is weakened
with doubt and loathing.
Resolutions of high expectations,
in a moment of overthinking turn away,
and lose the determination of standards.

Do not allow this to be,
be that which soars to the height deserved,
and let them fight to climb to your light . . .
and worship . . .

For all my fellow sufferers of singlehood

Pouring After Midnight

I know that it's late,
that I should sleep.
Yet, still, the gate's
too open to keep
worries that fate
has planted deep.

Dreams bring them to mind;
stars witness my strain;
in darkness I find
an ease to the pain;
I pour out the wine;
listen to the rain.

After midnight struck,
long before new day . . .
I become unstuck,
time has lost its sway . . .
I just need some luck,
get back on my way.

Better Than . . .

If you can pay attention for longer than
the length of a new YouTube video;
If you can remember what I'm telling you
in this first verse by the time of the last;
If you can wait, patient, for an answer
to your question that will take us off task;
If you can accept that others might matter too,
attention span not too long, not too short.

If you can accept your teachers do mean well,
can believe adults do know more than you;
If knowing, choose to listen just a little,
possibly finding something of value.
If you can wait to be taught any new skill
before you declare you'll never do it;
If you can help, and accept help from others,
without assuming this is a weakness.

If you can venture far outside your comfort zone,
trying something you've never tried before;
If you can be vulnerable and open
and not shrink into your shell when you're caught;
If you can be there for others, ev'n when they
were not always there for you in your need;
If you can show your feelings, like pain, fear, love . . .
and never regret letting people in.

If you can learn enough to know you don't know,
and continue to learn until you do;
If you can not flaunt your ignorance too clear,
and believe you can always learn more.
You might just be better than we ever were,
learning from our mistakes, and your own;
looking back, looking forward, take it all in,
and — more to the point — you might save us all.

For the post millennials   – 31 –

Oh, Come On! I Was Just!

That bit, where you stop
and stare

at nothing

because you started
and then stopped
and then started
about ten different tasks
because you were just . . .

I'm sorry . . .
What was I saying?
Oh! right,
course I was just . . .
going to the loo,
and then I had to
start the coffee,
then put that glass,
that dish
over there.

The phone rang,
and I was going to
call you
earlier...
because I saw this thing
that reminded me of
that thing
you know, from when...

But then
that song came on
and by the time it finished
I forgot
that I needed
the loo so...

I'm Just,
going to

go.

What Can't You Do?

Can you help one person lift groceries
to their door, just one?
Yes, you can.

Can you solve world hunger,
far and near?
No, you can't.

Can you place essentials, now and then,
In the food bank of your local?
Yes, you can.

Can you house all the homeless
Provide every blanket and bed?
No, you can't.

Can you "see" them, and know them,
Respect their existence?
Yes, you can.

Can you solve mental health,
Heal all the sick of soul?
No, you can't.

Can you share your pain with someone,
Be vulnerable and open?
Yes, you can.

Can you make all people less mean,
Less thoughtless, cruel?
No, you can't.

Can you choose not to be mean,
Thoughtless and cruel?
Yes, you can.

Can you choose to stand up against
Those who're thoughtless, cruel?
Yes, you can.

Can you smile and tell your friend,
"It will be okay," when it might not?
Yes, you can.

Can you be there when it isn't okay,
With sympathy, kindness and tissues?
Yes, you can.

Can you change your look overnight,
To pure beauty, ideal?
No, you can't.

Can you find the beauty in your look,
Unique, and its own "flaws"?
Yes, you can.

Can you find the beauty in others,
Make sure they see it?
Yes, you can.

Can you fix everything by yourself,
For everyone, everywhere?
No, you can't.

Can you give time, attention and skill,
To a cause, an idea?
Yes, you can.

Can you control everything, everywhere,
Make it run perfect and smooth?
No, you can't.

Can you do small things, every day,
As and when you see?
Yes, you can.

There are a million big things,
We can't control or do.
We know we can't.

There are billions of small things,
We can choose to do.
We know we can.

Do what you can, when you can,
Accept what you can't, when you can't
We all can.

Reap and Sow

Plant the seeds that you wish to grow.
Don't waste effort on things you'll never see.
Risk the impossible, or never know.

Put your best out there, and not just for show.
Make e'ry word, e'ry sound all it can be.
Plant the seeds that you wish to grow.

Put passion paramount, a radiant glow.
Lead others to their light, to be truly free.
Risk the impossible, or never know.

For others to catch it, first we must throw.
Ideas are like acorns of the strongest tree.
Plant the seeds that you wish to grow.

Faster and faster time comes, watch it go.
Join in or be past, no matter your plea.
Risk the impossible, or never know.

Future unwritten, all must learn to sow.
Together we'll change things, together the key.
Plant the seeds that you wish to grow,
Risk the impossible, or never know.

You Are Enough

So many expectations
of what we must be,
schedules and appointments,
time makes us flee.
Racing through our lives,
too fast to see ...

You are enough ...

This week I'm too heavy,
this month too thin.
My hair's too short, too long,
blonde, red, brown can't win.
Too much make-up, not enough,
judgement makes a din ...

You are enough ...

In the gym for the perfect form.
But be sure to make time
for friends and work and family man,
being the breadwinner is also fine.
Be sporty and laddish, emotion too.
No tempers, tough and kind ...

You are enough ...

Be sexy not slutty, maternal not nagging,
perfect home and perfect job too . . .
Be assertive but not aggressive;
stay in the place we give you.
But break the ceiling, role model,
be all and nothing through and through.

You are enough . . .

When they say it's not enough
say, "Go to hell!"
Do what you can as well as you can
No one can tell.
Be the best human you know how,
Don't become a shell.

You are enough . . .

For Thea

Photo by: @simbailey.photography

Between

Gripping the line,
suspended between
moments of strain
danger might be
either side
but here is safety.

Golden glances
in the setting sunlight
holding fast
the barbed wire
above field fences.
Freedom unconfined.

Bright joy found
between field and flight,
between dusk and night,
in a moment of rest
under blue sky
soaring paused.

For Simon

Burst of colour
surrounded by sharp spikes.
Ow! beauty's danger.

Don't Wanna!

I cannot teach my class today
poor long-suffering teachers say,
I have pain, as well as a strain ...
a fluke a flux, so tell me plain ...
do I look sick, do I look well?
My vision's going, I can tell.
My planner's gone, forever lost ...
maybe it's with the garbage tossed.
Oh! You found it, now ... let me see —
Ugh ... no, no, no this just can't be,
that's all from last term's work, it's gone!
I knew that was too easy won ...
I think I might be getting plagues
the kind that knocks you out for days,
I'll cough and choke, it's just no good.
If I come in, I know I could
disease the school, I'll really try
to get in tomorrow, might cry ...
That wouldn't be helpful to show
the joy of words, to watch it grow,
more like weeds, they're everywhere!
Shouting, kicking, tantrums that flare.
I could not, should not dare come in,
my doctor says I'm way too thin,
I ate too much, it's poison sure,
I cannot possibly endure ...
a class of teens ... what did you say?
You say today is Saturday?
Hey! Wait up, drinks? I'm on my way!

Nope! Not Today!

2am, ugh, ok, paracetamol . . .

3am, really? Should have . . . zzzzzz

4am, ok this has to stop now,
I get yesterday was rough,
but really
enough is enough

6am, thanks . . . two hours
instead of one . . .
still, this repetition sours.

7am, OKAY! I admit it
no more coughing,
no more fever,
no more dizzy,
I give up, I'll call work . . .

Zzzzzzzzzzzzzzzzzzzzzzzzzzzzzzzzzzzzzz . . . .

Pass Me By

The minutes
pass to hours,
the hours
pass to days.

My life just
passes by
in more than
a few ways.

I forgot
how to smile.
I let slide
how to dance.

I just shop
and pay bills,
move through rooms,
just by chance.

A routine
helps me live,
gets me by
have my say.

Survive time,
only just.
I just wish
there's a play.

Stop the car,
pause the tape,
hold the line,
take the wheel.

Miss dancing,
miss laughing,
want to live
want to feel.

Take my hand
and stop me,
one minute
of pure will.

Take my hand
and hold me,
make some time
to stand still.

Don't leave me
to linger,
lose myself
Asking, "Why?"

Pass the time
by my side,
be here ... don't
pass me by.

Mama's Vanity

I don't know why it's so clear,
the memory of glinting light...
maybe it's because the owner was dear,
maybe because they remind me of night.

I would sit and watch in awe,
the bristles' sound with each stroke,
plain hair into liquid gold, raw
sparkling waves, beyond regular folk.

In the day I was tempted to lift
the mirror or comb, engraved brush.
But too heavy for my little fingers' grip,
afraid to break or get caught in a rush.

Many years ago that was for me;
though only a day or two it seems.
Sitting at her desk, it's my mother I see,
her hand still brushing my hair, in little girl dreams.

For my mother, Janet

Plague

Is there any point
in keeping you away?
If I cancel plans
will it stay at bay?

All the Lemsip in the land
all the cough drops in the sea
won't keep the bugs in hand.
T-minus two days to teach.

Talking with no voice,
all I can think is
teaching leaves no choice...
down with plans, be gone

Keep your plague far from me
stay home, stay warm,
and we will just see.
Maybe I won't get it...

Saturday, 4th January 2020
In the irony of all ironies, this was made and named
for a particularly bad post New Year's cold.

Washing Me Out

Clunk and clatter, as it goes round and round...
ev'ry time the clothes pile up I fear
that rattle, that grumble, that horrid sound...
this machine, this thing, just brings me to tears.
Reset the boiler, again and again...
hot water is needed, just help me out!
One device, just one, to not be a pain...
so I don't get a headache, scream and shout.
There's no winning against these machines, Blast!
Now the dryer's packed up, when will this end!
I've had more than enough, this is the last,
I need clean clothes, this drives me round the bend!
    The launderette, with promise of freedom, calls.
    Good thing too, this machine drives me up walls.

For the student who challenged me to write one about a broken washing machine when I told them a sonnet could be written about anything.

Sunday Admin

Recharge at 100%
time to belt in,
and belt up,
wind up for the week.
Did I finish
that letter?
Did I remember
to fold
the laundry?
Where did I put
that folder
I needed
for that thing
at 9am?

Ok, time for coffee...

annnnnd breathe...

Ready for more,
ready for lunch,
ready for tv,
ready for Monday...

Almost...

In the Wind

It whispers, softly, as it rushes past.
It tells you not to miss it as it goes.
It reminds you that nothing true can last.
It speaks of joy or pain, though no one knows.
Memory is fleeting ... treasure it now.
Memory lives forever ... in the wind.
Memory doesn't die ... it can grow.
Memory only waits for us to find.
Time will do both things, it lives, and it dies.
Time calls all of us, past us all ... it cries.

Your Exit

If you cannot support me my dear,
through all the bad, as well as the good,
This is your exit, right over here.

If you look only to unload fear;
I might suffer what you never could;
If you cannot support me my dear.

Loyalty to my trust must be clear...
telling others what you never should?
This is your exit, right over here.

There are those who will dry all my tears,
I can be loved, held and understood,
If you cannot support me my dear.

If you want to rage as I disappear,
since I will not stand one more falsehood,
This is your exit, right over here.

I choose better friends to draw me near,
Your loss and regret will be withstood
If you cannot support me my dear...
This is your exit, right over here.

For my friend Cat

Remaining

Such a little thing.
We must have forgot.
A dim light we all bring.
Seeing each other's lot.
What we all leave behind.
The things that get in the way.
The power we all find.
When someone asks, "Mind if I stay?"

Company Coming

On no! is that the time?
When's she coming? I knew
leaving it to morning...never fine!
Now there's way too much to do...

Dishes from last night...
okay, maybe from before...
okay, a week ago, alright,
at least I'm not making more.

Too busy to eat until this...
this...what is it? Laundry pile,
sigh, a cleaner would be bliss,
the vacuum hasn't worked in a while.

Company coming, I know she won't care,
but my mother would die of shame.
Now I run round, what goes where?
Things in the corner ask for a name.

I swear this isn't day to day.
I know I can get it done, I'll start
in a frenzied methodical way,
hmm, where did I put the cart?

Traces

A trace of you lingers here,
on the pillow next to mine,
and in my mind, it's still clear . . .
the comfort we always find.
Though you're gone for today,
what we have still remains,
where 'forever' isn't in the way,
nothing needs to be explained.
I turn, breathe in deep of you,
wrap myself in sheets we shared.
Calm created through and through,
with a friend who always cared.
No demands, no need to claim,
just company, no more or less.
Just relaxing, the only aim,
with talk and touch and kiss.
A trace of a smile on my face,
a trace of memory in my dream
always remains in this place,
always exactly what it seems.

For J —

Let Me See

Build your wall...
I'll tear it down
(both big and small).
Each stone I'll crack,
each line I'll cross,
no going back.
Each cloth will tear,
paint layers stripped,
till you stand bare.
Clutch hands to chest,
it matters not...
goes as the rest.

LET ME SEE!

Now I stand before you...
as you shake,
e'en so I look right through.
I'll take down my wall,
melt them away
both big and small.
I strip the paint,
I tear the cloth,
I stand and wait.
I wait to breach,
-that which you hold-
my hands outreached...

SO LET ME SEE...

The last stronghold.
The heart of you.
Last story told.
Both mind and soul,
all open now...
at no great toll
for I'm open too.
So, let it go
between me and you.
All can be now,
fear washes away
just let it flow...

AND LET ME SEE

Dishes in the Sink

We've all done it, just one glass
or just one plate, sitting
by the sink.
The breakfast bowl, rushing out the door
or just dessert, too late
before bed.
Maybe the casserole, needs a soak . . .
or just the pots, can wait
until tomorrow.
Before long the build-up stares,
stubbornly refusing to magically
be clean by itself.
Adding, one at a time, seems only
to add new plant species, growing
in the kitchen.
Now the stacks are daunting enough
that tackling it waits until a weekend . . .
with free time.
On the weekend, I find I have
more things demanding my time
than dishes.
Monday comes again and the dishes remain . . .
heavier, higher, more disgusting,
more repellent.
I want to wash them, I really do,
I want to clear it from my list
of things hanging.
Simplest things can wait, can't they?
Until they stack so high, heavy,
and crash, breaking you.

One Hundred Hands

Echoes come to me, through ages of time,
though long gone, they feel as if they're all mine.
With a single touch, lives before me play,
imprints go beyond mere mortar and clay.
    One hundred hands have passed this way;
    Touch them, hear, what they have to say.

Spirits caught in ev'ry corner and block,
memory preserved and timelessly locked.
Meeting forbidden, still two lovers kiss;
the touch of it all . . . I'm afraid to miss.
    One hundred hands have passed this way;
    Touch them, hear, what they have to say.

A mosaic of moments, years go by . . .
minstrel's song, king's war and a mother's cry.
Some memories are dark, painful to touch,
death and destruction, when sorrow's too much.
    One hundred hands have passed this way;
    Touch them, hear, what they have to say.

Rebuilding after is the way of life,
happiness valued, if the cost is strife.
Renewing brick by brick, hearth, home and gate.
One hundred hearts slowly woven by fate.
 One hundred hands have passed this way;
 Touch them, hear, what they have to say.

In unending circles, we build and break,
hundreds of hands... hundreds of lives at stake.
Day to day, year to year, we live and die;
a hundred times, we're watching how time flies.
 One hundred hands have passed this way;
 Touch them, hear, what they have to say.

For all those who came before, and after,
touch and share their hope, their joy, their laughter.
Mourn where one has fallen and where one stands
feeling in the walls hundreds of their hands.
 One hundred hands have passed this way;
 Touch them, hear, what they have to say.

F'in Rice

Why, why can't I get it?
Watered and measured,
still no good to fit
food most treasured,

Rice

F'in Rice!

I burn or I drown,
soggy white paste,
I fret and I frown,
ugh what a waste!

Rice

F'in Rice!

Dinner for 12? Sure!
multiple different dishes . . .
no matter what it's for
but no help for wishes

with rice!

F'in rice!

Neat rows man made,
wind buffeted fields,
volcanic leavings.

Fractured

An indescribable sound, a slow . . . brittle . . . breaking.
It happens in the dark, beneath the surface,
under the skin, under the muscle, no matter strength.
Deep in the bone, in the core, a small crack . . .
hardly noticeable at first, just enough to grind.
It could be a door that won't open,
It could be a door that won't close.
You push and you pull till your hands are raw,
till the blisters break and bleed, still you claw.
It could be a memory that is lost.
It could be a memory that is found.
Precious and elusive, sought after in the pathways,
firing neurons betray, keeping from you what's wanted.
Nightmarish trauma, behind every closed lid,
turning shadows to demons, demons to saviours;
until you can no longer tell if memory is past.
It could be the fear of always being alone.
It could be the terror of always being watched.
Like all things, too much or too little,
poison or palliative, crushing isolation or
the weight of constant company's expectations.

The crack splinters wider, deeper, darker.
The small grinding becomes a grating, gripping
distraction, crying, calling every thought.
It could be a helplessness; no options, no fight.
It could be too much choice with no clear track.
To depend completely on another, for life,
for death, for health, for wealth, lost, losing.
To be responsible for others, to have to make
choice after choice, life and death on a word.
Your word. Responsible for one, or one hundred.
Helping and helpless, is there much between?
The fracture becomes crippling, not seen, felt.
It shatters, splinters, crippling, crumbling.
The mind trapped behind a door in the dark...
with no memory, isolated and helpless.
Forgets when they felt anything else,
felt anything else but fractured and
fragmented, in sanity all it takes is one,
a single crack made brittle by the world.

Lost

Though I've been here many times,
I seem to have lost my way.
Light fades and apprehension climbs,
as the sun sinks at close of day.

Just as the rim sinks in the west,
the edge of the path finds me . . .
not long now till I can rest . . .
if the night doesn't blind me.

Roots trip my feet, branches snag,
leaves whisper secrets all around.
Each moment I'm lost seems to drag,
'If I fall, will I be found?'

Stars are hidden in the fog,
life is shrieking in the brush,
I see demons in a knotted log,
spirits in the breezes rush.

I desperately cry, 'Let me go!'
A distant glow not seen before,
floating flame, I'll never know,
it doesn't matter anymore.

Bad Medicine

It leaves a bitter taste
when asked by someone...
who should know better.
Unsympathetic,
unknown,
ignorant of reasons.
Just knowing
in her nursely opinion,
I 'ought' to want
children.
Just knowing
it's her nursely right,
to ask, 'don't' I?
Just biting my tongue,
I answer, "No"
and get my pill,
enraged.

Vicarious Shame

I am not proud
of a history that said,
for hundreds of years,
'You are property,
bought and sold.'
Treated like animals;
bred and beaten,
as less than I,
a pale shadow.

I am not proud
of laws that said
if you could not read
you could not vote . . .
when we never taught
the value of words
to those too valuable
to let free of
a pale shadow.

I am not proud
of those who said,
'Separate but Equal'
was good enough,
without enough
of anything that might
educate . . . instead of
segregate. Learning only
a pale shadow.

I am not proud
that a threat
to financial pride...
"Black Wall Street",
destroyed 35 blocks,
hundreds, thousands,
of lives...livelihoods...
They armed and deputised
a pale shadow.

I am not proud
that team pride
stands by the place,
the neighbourhood,
where you live.
Baseball diamonds
only value a colour
with more talent than
a pale shadow.

I am not proud
that even in war,
the ultimate sacrifice,
the colour of skin
seemed to matter
more than the colour
of blood, given freely.
Uniform honour seems
A pale shadow.

I am not proud
that four policemen
could walk away
from beating someone
for 15 minutes;
with video and 15 more
watching them do it.
Justice it seems is
a pale shadow.

I am not proud
that at 14 I learned
the world stops to hear
if a black sports star
killed his white wife.
But at 12 I didn't know
about genocide in a
black country, unimportant
to a pale shadow.

I am not proud
that I never read
the words of brilliance,
poems and prose,
of all colours.
The decision not mine,
but mine the gap . . .
all my reading of only
a pale shadow.

I am not proud
that no matter how badly
I want to be
a good ally,
how ashamed I get,
Vicariously, of them . . .
it feels like ashes.
Like it can only ever
a pale shadow.

I am not proud
we allowed him, them,
to represent us
to the world, be seen . . .
as if their hate
is all we are, were,
would ever be. Humanity
forever remaining
a pale shadow.

I am not proud
a movement of protest
is still necessary,
still shunned,
still blamed, somehow
for the ignorance,
for the murders
committed casually by
a pale shadow.

I am not proud
that too many names,
too many incidents,
are completely unknown.
Not seen, not shown,
not heard...
by me or anyone
who looks like me...
a pale shadow.

I am not proud.
My own ignorance
overwhelms me.
The sheer weight,
of the weight
that people carry...
just to exist
makes me ill...
a pale shadow.

Don't Accept

Don't accept, "Because that's the way it's always been done."
As a reason to keep people down, it's always been true,
Goodwill of the many can overcome the evil of "some."

Imbalance of justice, where it seems prejudice won,
Where the system is fought by the brave, no matter how few,
Don't accept, "Because that's the way it's always been done."

Rights gained and held, for small groups, one by one, by one.
Each voice and ally, adds strength; add me, add you . . .
Goodwill of the many can overcome the evil of "some."

Stand up and say, "No!" when what's wrong then, now, is wrong to come.
Shout till you can't even when shouting seems all you can do . . .
Don't accept, "Because that's the way it's always been done."

Together change happens, from highest high rise to lowest slum,
Make them change, and change, don't stop till it's pushed through,
Goodwill of the many can overcome the evil of "some."

Tragically, evil persists, when too many good people get too numb
Be alive, be feeling, be fiery, do what's hardest to do.
Don't accept, "Because that's the way it's always been done."
Goodwill of the many will always overcome the evil of "some."

Ignite

A fire begins with an ember, glowing in the dark.
A flare, a flicker, glints in the breath before breath.
A multitude of voices begin with a single spark.
Whispers rustle, kindle, stir the flames of the rest.

Styles stimulate and animate another, then another.
Once set off, flame spreads many threads of light,
like a web connected, the whole world covered.
Out of silence beams a symphony so bright.

Before us we scatter the fragments of voices,
granules of soul set in motion, with rich soil.
Sifting through leaves of paper, many choices . . .
burn the past to ashes with our tears and toil.

A place for everything and everything in place,
we dredge the earth and grime, find our grit.
Fire and Dust burns with us all face to face,
facing the cinders of the truth we have writ.

First Published in 'Spirit of Fire & Dust' Anthology, Allographic Press 2021

At the Zoo

Running around in a confined space,
caged and bound so much of the time.
When out in the compound, naturally
they run wild, in their constructed habitat.
The silver fox is cool, calm, experienced...
no need to be showy or bark loud.
He knows how to hunt without hunting,
To wait till the pups tire themselves.
The hyenas' bark clashes, echoes, deafening...
they run in packs, some girls, some boys.
But, girls or boys, the night is punctuated
by sudden, grating, laughter at nothing.
The young wolf, not yet grizzled,
slopes through the paths, carefree.
Unassuming, light stepped, with hungry eyes,
waiting till no one's looking to close in.
The mama bear, pawing around food and drink,
patient with cubs as they stumble.
But when they stumble too far, or stray
too close to the young wolf...look out!
The songbird, keeping all spellbound,
voice floating, filling the skies, inspiring
the other animals to join in, as best they can.

Sadly, not all have the gift, even if they think they do.
The indecisive sloth, standing, moving slower than
a frozen river . . . making all wait behind him.
Watching fumbling fingers take forever to find
the coloured leaves, so he can move on, so all can.
The loud and lazy lion, his pride around him,
roaring as the females fetch food to sustain.
The mane displayed in careless show, dominant,
but no more than the peacock's plumage.
The Praying Mantis, her hunt in full flow
seeks a mate and a meal for the night.
Men she enjoys should beware, for the close
they might be left with less than they might choose.
The mocking jay, swaying and saying his "truth",
declaring his fitness, seeking nectar, more and more.
None are convinced though he strut and he shout.
It's amazing patience the other animals don't throw him out.
It's wild and vibrant this urban zoo,
In most I see me, and I see you.
Animals we were, are, will forever be,
As we are our own keepers, we have the key.
Consider your display, attract the right attention.
Otherwise your caricature next, I might mention.

Feeling It

Electric eyes, across the room, no one else there.
Every nerve ending crackles, all my blood seems aflare.
Before the first touch, before I catch breath, before I think.
The thought takes over, crossing the room I blink.
My lids seem to be in slow motion, their own free will.
Like a sleepy cat my bedroom eyes hold us so still.
I run hands through my hair, strands fall where they may,
Nails tease my lips, half open, more than words can say.
Fingertips along my jaw, trace the lines of my face,
Take your time . . . and mine, there's no need to race.
Sounds of the bar, fade, I can't help but hear
Pounding fire, beat round my soul . . . with you so near.
Sense of time joins the other senses, gone far away,
Speech without words, volumes spoken with nothing to say
Let this moment last, I silently cast in hopeful heart,
Let it happen, just once as it seems, let it just start.

I Miss...

I miss my dream of you, which isn't fair,
my hopes, for us, for what we might have been,
were girlish dreams, made without enough care
for a real you, instead of what I'd seen
in books, on screens... fairytale love in mind.
I saw what I wanted to see, no more.
Didn't see you, just expected to find
that you wanted the same; I was so sure.
I miss the idea we'd love forever,
I miss the thought you'd need me as I you,
I miss the hope that we'd never sever,
I miss believing all said would be true.
I miss my dream of us, though never real.
Can't help hoping, dreaming, that love to feel.

At the Door

I feel alive, at the door
To my home, my own...
With my kittens waiting
In the front window.
A calm settles on me.
Here I am most me.
I feel alive as it's a life
I have chosen, I choose,
Every day, as I arrive,
To my home, my own...

I feel alive, at the door
To write, labour of love...
With my students waiting
In my class, at their desks.
A determination invigorates me,
Here I am not just me.
I feel the weight of those I teach
I feel the weight of those who taught,
The need to help, each time,
To work, labour of love...

I feel alive, at the door...
To the station, travelling...
With a new place, going
Where I've never been.
A thirst inspires me,
Here I grow me.
I feel curious, of it all,
I look, hear, smell, taste a life.
Any day I go somewhere, anywhere,
To the station, travelling.

I feel alive, at the door
Of somewhere, I don't want to go,
With the doctor, or lawyer, or boss
Waiting with unknown news.
Anxiety energizes me,
Here can throw me.
I feel out of control, but
I face that fear, alive.
Every time I must,
To somewhere I don't want to go.

I feel alive, at the door
Where my friends gather . . .
Whatever the reason, number,
Wherever we're gathering.
Companionship and empathy,
In joy or sorrow we are we.
I feel social life surround,
The company I keep defines
The kind of person I am
Where my friends, gather . . .

I feel alive, at the door
To my home, my parents',
With my family waiting
All together, all in love,
A comfort fills me, unconditional
Here I began to be me.
I feel as me as is possible
I have memories, like a blanket,
Any time it's always there
In my home, my parents'.

Ode to Points of Light

Tradition's call each year we heed
bringing out these evergreens
whether fake or true it holds the seed
of what the season truly means.
My heart grows full as I place it there,
the string glowing warm, in branches deep,
carefully strung till all is lit throughout.
Stepping back to check the balance . . . it's fair,
memories of years at home softly creep
and I take up each piece as time spools out.
The ribbons, the bells, pictures of old;
baubles and icicles; dangling snowflakes;
with each ornament, each hook, my childhood told.
Some I found, some I bought, some makes,
some from years long gone, some yesterday.
All together, like the tree, how they grow.
Seeing each brightens my spirits, lifts
each thought, remembered like vision played.
To see and understand each, would be to know
all of my fondest seasonal times, like gifts.
As soon as December starts, I see it shine,
But come January, it's hard to let it go,
display of memory, all that makes them mine.
When it's packed away, I'm comforted to know
the closet will hold it less than a year,
delight is safe and sound, waiting for me
to unpack and relive, all that was before.
As time makes hope less and less clear,
I'm holding on to my tree so I can still see
each light remains bright, as I build more.

Careful, trusting
hands take the ornament,
tinkling tree lights.

The Back Steps

No one uses the front
except on holidays, maybe . . .
The comforting creak
under ancient maple shady.

When little, I held tight the hand
Of one or both parents for balance.
Slick with fall leaves or icy
never seemed worth the chance.

Sometimes the paint would be fresh,
sometimes it faded with wear.
Summers spent peeling corn ears,
or letting the dog out with care.

He used to run off if not watched.
If too cold, I would stand in the door.
No reason to lock the back here
this town still has some trust I'm sure.

I miss letting the cat in
I miss letting the dog out
I miss hip checking the door
I miss mom's "Come home!" shout.

But I know they still wait
In thought and in memory
The back steps of home welcome,
Will always be there for me.

The Card Game's Upstairs

My memories emerge at the news from home,
and so far away, thinking of them, I let them roam.
In a half dream I hear through the door
the clicking nails of Pepe from years before.
Aunt Anna swears and I hide my smiles.
All through years, we came miles and miles,
To enjoy the food and laughter heard
at Aunt Katie's houses, she always cared,
wherever she was to bring us to table.
There sits Aunt Mae, who was always able
to see my heart at the turn of the deck.
As Aunt Sass arrives, I just have to check,
whose cackle is whose as they sit around.
Until the matriarch is finally found . . .
at the head of the lot naturally.
Violet Hunsicker, the card queen actually.
All together we laugh and we cry,
in my dream I don't need to ask why,
playing games late into the night . . .
I wake renewed and know in the daylight
they're awaiting all of us, through our waiting tears,
I'm telling you, trust me, the card game's upstairs.

For Grandmom Hunsicker, Aunt Anna, Aunt Mae,
Aunt Katie and Aunt Sass

I Don't Want to Write About Lockdown (Part 1)

Everyone is reflecting
on the last
6 months
of not seeing
friends and family.
But thanks to
webcam programs
I've seen
more friends
more family
more often
than any other
6 months...ever.
Because people are
more willing
more available
more still
more aware
of how important
seeing is.

Over 24 weeks
of wondering
what next week
will bring...
of seeing the wishes
of people
who wanted
a never-ending
weekend
granted.
All blends together
until schedules
are lost
and the 172 days
begin to lose
their meaning
and I try to find
a reason to get up.

Everyone is reflecting
and writing
and reading
and knitting
and learning
new languages
new skills
new hobbies
new music
new films
new shows...
4,128 hours
of trying to fill
gaps previously filled
with the rat race
deadliness
appointments, alarms
and snooze buttons
too much time now
to know what we did.

I don't want to reflect
on how much
this isn't affecting me
as it should.
I don't want to write
about spending
247,680 minutes
not climbing the walls,
not missing
my commute,
not feeling put out
by not going out,
not feeling any more lonely
than usual,
not feeling guilt
about not learning
new skills
not finishing that unfinished novel
no guilt about
no guilt or interest.

If I don't think about
Lockdown,
If I don't write about
Lockdown,
I won't worry
about my heart
crying out alone
in these months
weeks, days, minutes
any more than
the decades of fellowship
and love
of family and friends
before now
(and hopefully after)
these 14,860,800 seconds
that have consumed
the consciousness
of the world
to the exclusion of millennia.

First Published in 'Life Inna Lockdown', 2020, Chapter 14

Title Poem

What we have all
endured

Coffee and Papercuts

January

The coffee brings me calm in the morning,
The papercuts should be fair warning.

First of the year began, as it does,
with the usual joy change brings.
Not being home, unusual, as it goes...
No family with me, the new year rings.

Overnight the news was ablaze,
Australia's suffering, before our eyes.
Humans *and* animals, tragically razed,
destroyed, as a helpless world cries.

A crisis brewed with explosive force,
Trump killed Solemani at Iraqi airport.
Near World War III, I'm thinking, "Of course..."
This year, only new begun, will be short.

The coffee brings me calm in the morning,
The papercuts should be fair warning.

Not the only war, in a year not yet old:
Libya, Yemen, Iran fires on not one but two,
Drone attacks and missiles, wreckage unfolds,
Downed planes and bases, killing the innocent too.

Missiles launched at hosts, soldiers the target,
why must bystanders pay for other's crimes?
Hundreds killed or shot down, all should regret,
amazed, *one week in*, as fear climbs and climbs.

Looking beyond, a summer intern finds,
With like minds, a planet system 4.4 billion aged.
Yet on Earth we can't seem to love our own kind,
Boko Haram, against Nigeria, 89 killed, not caged.

The coffee brings me calm in the morning,
The papercuts should be fair warning.

World loses its mind when royals retreat to reality
after decades of limelight telling them to.
But by mid-January reality retreats to the banality
Of multiple debates, to contrast a fool.

For only the second time in US history . . .
Articles of impeachment issued . . . and denied.
Why may always remain a mystery
Obstruction, abuse of power, little hope died.

Travel advisories issued but first US case shows
the shadow that would haunt, as long as it lasts.
A public health emergency, the W.H.O. knows,
those who don't . . . tragically, innocently, laugh.

Two exits end this January time;
Kobe, his daughter and seven more crash;
Official "Brexit" makes UK believe it will be fine
(though later it might seem the choice was rash).

For me the month ends in more personal vein,
for 20 years I've wanted my words out.
A friend of a friend publishes my refrain,
and from a simmering whisper my poems shout.

The coffee brings me calm in the morning,
The papercuts should be fair warning.

February

Trump acquits himself poorly in Union speech,
but the Senate acquits his impeachment without trial.
Boy Scouts are bankrupt as accusations reach.
First US recorded covid death fails to rile.

Ahmed Arbery goes for his morning jog,
with Georgia bigots not far behind,
shooting him in some crazy racist fog...
and so begins a fire that makes us blind.

Syria may still be at war, as it has before,
but NATO supports Turkey and the world breathes...
US and Taliban have a conditional peace, at its core
when troops are withdrawn and we hope none got left.

For me, a trip long planned and wanted finally arrives,
unaware of lockdown to come, I go to Rome and see
the heart of the eternal city that beats and thrives.
The seeds of *Chasing Apollo* are planted within me.

Never speak too soon, never count too far,
2020 already taught us to keep doors and windows open.
A leap year unlike any other, way off par,
After two months down, is the only direction sloping?

The coffee brings me calm in the morning,
The papercuts should be fair warning.

March

Democrats ask if an opponent for Trump can be found?
By March it's Biden or Bernie ready to clash,
Within the week Italy's lockdown has its first round.
Travel bans are climbing even as global markets crash.

With a pandemic declared, more than lives are lost.
Communities shut their borders one by one,
Spain, UK, EU, India ... Lockdown the cost
With sports and competitions closed, nothing's won.

Ahmed Arbery not yet out of mind ...
Breonna Taylor fans into a brighter flame.
Shot at home, police looked, but couldn't find ...
warrant for a mislabelled drug dealer, why they came.

The coffee brings me calm in the morning,
The papercuts should be fair warning.

A victory for victims, in the trial of movie man.
'Me Too' movement will not sit down, shut up or stop,
Weinstein sentenced; 23 years is the court plan.
How far abusers fall, when brought down from the top.

Half a million Covid cases by March's end,
with a third of the world in lockdown, jobs fall.
Unemployment everywhere, no one can pretend
that bankers and offices are the important ones after all.

The chain that binds us all, on which *all* our lives depend?
The *food* chain, the stockers of shelves, drivers bringing it.
Us teachers too, in the crossfire with kids, learning defends ...
shut down and moved to screens, ultimate teachers winging it.

This move to screens moves my family to weekly meetings...needed.
Knowing I won't be home for the foreseeable future, brings fear.
Getting the full program when, "and one more thing..." 2 minutes heeded,
strangely closer, while farther parted, in fact...never felt so near.

April

With worldwide millions ill and millions more going jobless,
The only April fools, unfortunately, are the ones in charge.
Trump leaves the WHO and touts medicine that's pointless.
Boris in hospital as every country's death toll's enlarged.

The coffee brings me calm in the morning,
The papercuts should be fair warning.

Disease tragically, obviously, can't stop wars or war crimes,
Islamist militants in Mozambique, Syrian army officers on trial.
Iran launches military satellite, like we're in Sci-fi times...
Space aims back with asteroid near miss only 4 million miles.

For those of us who grew up with "I want to believe"
space has been a focus and a fictional escape.
So, Pentagon releasing video clips to relieve
UFO mystery, confirmed our suspicions beyond red tape.

Stranger than fiction the thought of patriots at home,
laying siege to a Governor's house, threatening her life,
Where do they want to go? From where have they come?
That demanding lockdown's end will be anything but strife?

The coffee brings me calm in the morning,
The papercuts should be fair warning.

May

Dystopian nightmares continue "murder" hornets invading,
photographs in all the papers of the first visible black hole,
fossils show early man (earlier than thought) Bulgaria parading,
multi-national science finds a microbe, a cure for Malaria could unfold.

33 million unemployed and death toll; still on the rise
A world-wide mental health crisis we all felt.
Kabul sees funerals and maternity blown up in all eyes.
Annexing Jordan valley means Palestine's hand is dealt.

Nature also rages, Somalia has deaths in flash flood,
India evacuates millions as a cyclone tears and destroys,
cicadas expected, like the plagues, will it be withstood?
Between man and nature, all lives seem a toy.

Rich parents are caught out paying children's way,
unfair advantage finally called out and called down.
Twitter finally labels Trump "misleading", have to say,
a drop in the bucket, in floods of lies we may drain.

The coffee brings me calm in the morning,
The papercuts should be fair warning.

Arbery, Taylor and so many others, joined by fresh hell,
George Floyd, murdered slowly, while the world must watch.
Not a shout or a scream, but a whisper all too well,
"I can't breathe" sparked round the world like a match.

The world mourned, and it raged, and the shock
sparked Philadelphia, Atlanta and L.A. (*again*)
curfews did nothing to stop it, or block
the Black Lives Matter protests from being plain.

The coffee brings me calm in the morning,
The papercuts should be fair warning.

Egyptian and Zambian presidents pardon thousands,
but blowing up 46,000-year-old Australian caves, mining bought?
China criminalizes civil liberties, protesting, no taking stands.
While Costa Rica *gives* same sex marriage liberties, who could've thought?

Hope and despair mix, point and counterpoint, more than usual this year.
By now it's become a joke, a meme of dystopian and apocalyptic times.
My dream of being published among this, within all that fear,
and my birthday and promotion of dreams must be creative finds.

The coffee brings me calm in the morning,
The papercuts should be fair warning.

June

As the protests mount Trump threatens us with troops...
military against our own, on our soul, when we're *right.*
As if epidemic violence, and corona didn't have enough loops,
The Democratic Republic of Congo has a new Ebola fight.

Russian oil leak leaves 20,000 tons of Siberian plight.
Border skirmishes between India and China kill on both sides.
And while the DC Mayor designates Plaza to BLM fight,
Atlanta protests shooting of Rayshard Brooks, rage continues to ride.

Rayshard Brooks being added to the list seems beyond belief,
even as Mississippi retires the *last* confederate state flag,
but a blind Trump insensitivity to the past is no relief,
holding a rally of hate on Juneteenth in Tulsa, our optimism lags.

From rocked by stupidity, Mexico is rocked in reality,
A 7.5 earthquake strikes the coast killing four.
U.S. Supreme Court says laws fit, that someone's sexuality,
their orientation, is covered in Civil Rights of 50 years or more.

Here in England, the pressure is up, lockdown for everyone else fits . . .
But us teachers are desperate to get back, to help the kids who struggle.
Determined and lettered as "key" we join the transport in our risk,
Without education and socializing our youth will be left in a trouble.

The coffee brings me calm in the morning,
The papercuts should be fair warning.

July

Like Weinstein and Epstein before her Maxwell faces arrest.
The FBI fighting for those too young, gone or unable to have their say.
The state of Oregon sues their own government, a test,
To see if they can justify using federal troops to lock protesters away.

Floods in China and Nepal leave hundreds dead,
but it's into the millions for the homeless and missing.
Global cases top 15 million with no end ahead,
Extra judicial executions Burkina Faso, terror rising.

We go farther in space it seems, than here among our own.
NASA's successful rover mission to Mars looks to the stars.
Adding to his crazy . . . Trump must think outer space is his home,
with his wild idea to delay the election, is a desperate pitch too far.

The coffee brings me calm in the morning,
The papercuts should be fair warning.

Having missed my usual yearly visit, because of a family plan,
skip the one Christmas to go twice in one year I thought . . .
turns into a cancelled reunion, loss of an aunt . . . 2020 demands
the sacrifice of many Christmases to come to naught.

August

We watch in horror, as it was in January, in Australia's down under,
So it is in California, wildfires, heatwaves and thunderstorms,
I didn't know firenadoes existed, even astronauts stare in wonder,
fire breathing dragon of clouds, by end of month 1-million-acre burns.

In Beirut, Lebanon, disaster strikes though natural it is not,
Ammonium Nitrate explodes hundreds killed, thousands hurt,
Hundreds of thousands mourn the home they haven't got.
Leaving billions in damage, only a crater to show its worth.

In Belarus election results rejected by the opposition, protest sparking,
hundreds of thousands demanding their vote counts, demanding to be free.
In our free country a woman named candidate for Vice-president is walking
whereas elections past she was a slave, segregated, no vote, barely *be*.

Summers end in peace for some, Israel and UAE make their third deal.
Africa declared free of wild polio, second eradicated virus, pray for a third.
Pray for the same success with Ebola, with Covid . . . let science make it real.
Pray for similar successes, similar lives saved, other vaccines have turned.

The coffee brings me calm in the morning,
The papercuts should be fair warning.

Wisconsin protests over the shooting of Jacob Blake, take to the streets.
In counter a teen, with a gun he didn't need, shot two unchallenged, walked.
Who comes from a different state, defends shops of those he'd never meet?
Athletes take a stand, boycott sports, in protests their white fans balked.

A hero, a King, in Marvel's universe becomes a hero in our real one.
Chadwick Boseman kept his illness secret, until it took him from us,
the strength to fight so hard off screen while he fights on for our fun.
A need to burn bright while he could, and to go with a minimum fuss.

Oil spills again 2,000 tons, this time near islands, Japanese tanker.
Oily politician, Bannon, arrested for the fraud of money for a wall.
Trump continues to threaten the US postal service, like a canker,
In pandemic using the safety of the mail to vote, he might lose all.

The coffee brings me calm in the morning,
The papercuts should be fair warning.

September

Westcoast wildfires again cause pain and destroy,
2.1 million acres in and around LA constant burning,
Started by pyrotechnic to reveal a girl or boy,
Oregon ablaze, "forest management" is Trump's blaming.

A different fire burns, wanting names of police who shot
Dijon Kizzee the end of August, family justifiably crying out.
Shooting two deputies in their patrol car makes it burn hot,
There is no relief, no fire break, that will put these flames out.

A woman who served the highest court in the country 27 years,
a woman who ensured *women* had the use of their own voice . . .
has passed, at 87, a giant, a pillar, her exit brings sorrow and fears
to all those who worry at the successor, when it's *his* choice.

When Trump fills her seat, inviting many to a nomination event . . .
Covid infects attendees, maskless, ignorant or downright ignoring.
No surprise, with shouting insults clear debate conditions prevent,
No commitment to going quietly, after election, in peaceful transition.

The coffee brings me calm in the morning,
The papercuts should be fair warning.

The worthless warrant, that got innocent Breona Taylor killed
is supported by unsupportable decision not to go forward and try.
The police officers making the mistake, family understandably filled
with disbelief and confusion, as are we all, unable to fathom why.

Deadly clashes, elsewhere in the world, a quick cycle seems.
Armenians and Azerbaijani fight each other in war . . .
surely battling disease, hunger is enough to haunt our dreams?
Apparently not, when people *have* trouble they still ask for more.

I have returned to school, though most others still stay home,
Those with special needs don't get them all met that way.
Balancing personal fear, safety and benefit . . . myself compared to some.
Choosing to join key workers, going out into it every day.

October

Further results of a careless attitude to science and masks.
White House outbreak, from meetings and exposed groups.
Trump himself caught it despite various "cures" in various flasks.
His case added to the 8 million US, and misinformation loops.

The strange and the sad join the feed as the year declines . . .
Eddie Van Halen at 65 joins those gone but always remembered,
with Irish ruling Subway bread isn't bread, tax break denied,
with fluffy, venomous, Texas puss caterpillar, worry reaching December.

The coffee brings me calm in the morning,
The papercuts should be fair warning.

With a sensible cease fire in Armenia, Azerbaijan fight,
Some sense comes to a flare up from 13 days before.
A sense *Michigan* could use, to recall what is right.
FBI arrests 13 *men* trying to kidnap their governor . . . what more?

November

This month is dominated by equal parts hope and fear . . .
of that which the intelligent and the desperate *need* to have.
Elections for one don't usually affect so many near or far,
four years of irrational, unbelievable behavior . . . may (finally) leave.

Or not . . . he declares a win, demands mail-in votes stop being counted,
No one stops counting, keeping safe but using our vote to make a change.
Trump resists and brings lawsuits, as the opposing votes mounted . . .
Pennsylvania, Georgia, Michigan, major news . . . all ready to turn the page.

Too short for a page, 240 characters fires the Secretary of Defense, on whim.
Telling battle ground states to ignore what their voters call a result,
Declaring he'll only leave White House when Biden "officially" replaces him.
Near month's end when transition team has access, seems an insult.

Science provides a choice and possibilities of "normality's" return.
Worldwide effort, best minds, labs do what they can, though questions call.
Trying to make working vaccines from what they can and have learned.
Doses will roll out, sleeves will roll up, we choose and hope numbers will fall.

Some science mysteries might never be solved though.
Discovered and reported, metal monoliths around the world.
Over 200 made or found, Sci-fi inspired? Alien? Who knows!
An enigma we should savor though it never be unfurled.

We must make sure our answer is in question form,
when considering another cultural loss to what we know.
What is, the loss of Alex Trebeck from Jeopardy we mourn?
On the daily double we bet we would *never* be ready for him to go.

The coffee brings me calm in the morning,
The papercuts should be fair warning.

Thanksgiving felt like a self-contradiction for the first time,
20 years living abroad, only twice have I not gathered into the room
friends near and far all parts of life, gifts I'm honored to call mine.
But now, this year, no choice . . . only place I gather for thanks . . . Zoom.

But as with family in March, like all the lessons we have learned,
a surprising benefit came from jumping to the video mode.
Anyone from any time in my life, could join, space time spurned.
Everyone's lighter, connected, further, easier with just simple code.

December

Weeks of tantrums lead an AG to claim voter fraud is the trick.
As protests and mishandling of lockdown continue everywhere.
The Supreme Court hears Texas talk of nullifying four states' votes . . . sick.
It's rejected and the Electoral College confirms, hope begins to flare.

Both the UK and US, really in the whole suffering world, healing starts.
Tragically, after more than 1.69 million global passings, we have all felt loss.
But as the year that halted the world closes, there is a light to our hearts,
on the solstice the "Christmas star" not seen in 800 years, touches frost.

The only way to keep my family, friends, students and self safe, stay home.
From technology, sat on the couch, I watch them play, sing and enjoy lights.
Having endured so much, and in full knowledge there will be more to come,
all that is left is to know we can hold on, keep a return to all in our sights.

The coffee brings me calm in the morning,
The papercuts should be fair warning.
May we all find joy in the darkest day,
May we all find the words we need to say.

Prose

Full sentence musings,
thoughts shared

A Good Night

Oh, so worth it. I ache everywhere but it was a good night. Time for the recovery, pick up the dress . . . where is the hanger? Ugh, I'll find it later. Comb through the pile of discards from 3am, dump out the purse, put the sparkly butterfly hair clips that got taken out at 11:30 away in their holder, put the jewellery back in the jewellery box . . . where is that earring? Somewhere between Covent Garden and Southwark, I guess. Time to stand the shoes upright, throw out the tights (some things can't be salvaged) and unplug the curling iron. Coffee, I need coffee, and food, and Advil.

Looking through the pictures, God it was a good night. I felt great from the minute I stepped out my door. I planned my look for months, more effort put into my outfit than I have since senior prom, which is ironic since the butterflies and the handbag were from that 18-year-old's outfit. I got more compliments, more double takes, more stares that I can remember in a long time. There were smiles and laughter with friends, a beautiful dance show followed by fun (non-professional) dancing at the club, ringing in the New Year.

New Year, new decade . . . it should feel different, shouldn't it? As I walked and walked (and walked) to the nearest open tube station, I kept thinking about that, took my mind off cold feet. The decade that was ending had fewer good memories than bad, some unpleasant and unpredictable changes I would rather not have experienced. So now, it should feel new, right? I still felt great, still riding the night of laughter and smiles, but I wanted to feel something other than the long (seemingly endless) walk. I have this project, planned and considered, the one you're reading now: 'Poems and musings, one a day, whatever comes out for a whole year.' Yeah I know, it was my idea and even I think it feels pretentious.

Maybe not, we all have those stray thoughts and daydreams. We all see the little image that pops in our head when we hear a song on our music player or smell the grilled onions for the sausage stand outside a train station. What we all also have is that feeling of isolation at times; maybe not all the time, but it's there … sometimes even in a crowd. I decided there, on the bridge over the Thames, that I would share mine with you. In the cold dark of the (very) early morning, the first hours of the year, walking off the last drinks of the party, and wishing I'd brought flat shoes in a bag, that I would share those thoughts … those musings, those poems, those images, those snatches of half-forgotten memories.

Yes I know, it's still pretentious … so what? I'm a poet, a writer, I'm supposed to be pretentious. So I'll put on another coffee pot, sit down today, and tomorrow, and the next day. You can stop reading whenever you want, I won't be offended, get up from the café table whenever and come back later when you're not too busy. Share one back with me, in your mind, get a fresh start and laugh or cry or turn your nose up. Do what you gotta do, me I've got to share this year and indulge this project. Just keep the coffee pot full and mind the papercuts, they sting sometimes.

January 1st, 2020

Looking Over My Shoulder

It's kind of a trap, that whole New Year thing. Fresh start, fresh date, stale resolutions. Now that it's a decade it's almost worse. People reflect (which is good I suppose) on the last ten years as it turns over from 19 to 20 ... I even fell for it myself. For, perhaps, a minute.

All it took was one brief reminiscence of some key dates to realise, this last decade was the most difficult in existence to date for me. Lots of change, like everyone, growing: mentally, emotionally, horizontally ... like everyone. Not all change is good, and not all reflecting or obsessing on change is good. Maybe it's not all good for me. Sometimes things that are technically bad for us are needed, there are bad days that require chocolate ... there are really bad days that require Bloody Marys. But actually searching a cumulative abyss for meaning just makes you squint.

Instead of trying to make sense of all I have lost the last ten years; of trying to justify it or balance it with what I've gained and revel (by posting such musings on social media) in the 'balance' of it; the give and take ... I resolved to, well, not. My own personal rebellion, no looking back. Mostly because I can't be sure the books are balanced; and if they're not (in either direction) I'm not sure I want to analyse why they're not. Not sure I want to steep my thoughts in blame or arrogant aggrandisement. I want to progress by not regressing, make a conscious choice to not overthink before and spend my energy on now and next. Some people may need it, but I find this time, I'm pretty sure I need to not look over my shoulder anymore.

Thursday, 2nd of January 2020

Falling Off Horses

Like all children with summer camp memories, mine are half based on what I recall and what my parents tell me. What I can clearly remember from my 10-year-old horse-riding experience is that it is easier to fall off than you think.

Walk, trot, canter class was doing well. It's difficult to remember a time when I was small and light enough to bounce around, but I do remember my foot bouncing out of the stirrup. I desperately tried to keep from falling off but should have prioritised making the horse stop over hanging onto the saddle. Slowly, as my horse continued a few strides, I slid down until I was hanging off the side of the horse by the saddle. It felt like forever until my instructor noticed; I had just begun to wonder if I might be better off letting go and hitting the ground.

Still you know what they say? "Get back on the horse!" Well, I didn't have another opportunity until I was bought a hack, a trail ride, for my 21st birthday. This time I was the 'experienced' rider, while my partner was the 'new' rider. I was amused that he kept getting pulled forward by the reins when his horse wanted to eat the weeds. I would feel better about being amused if, halfway through the ride, I hadn't felt myself slipping from the saddle once again.

Now I was feeling quite abashed and as if karma had asserted itself. Once again I made the mistake of assuming my foot had slipped from the stirrup and that clinging to the saddle was a better idea than trying to stop the horse. I believe that this time it might have worked, if not for the realisation as I grabbed the saddle's pommel that it was also moving. Turns out the saddle had been improperly secured and the horse had stopped puffing out its chest, allowing the looser, more comfortable, girth to dump me unceremoniously on the ground. Directly at the feet of the horse and the partner I had felt so superior to at the start. The most difficult part was not eating humble pie, it was making sure I didn't laugh at myself so loudly I startled the horse into trampling me.

Sometime after that I met a fellow teacher who owned two horses. Endurance riding is not a sport I feel equal to, but helping my friend exercise both horses at once with a Sunday ride through the Kent countryside was an effort I was more than happy to do as often as we could manage.

One brisk October morning, we were on a ride enjoying the fact that we were off the following week for half term. I may have gotten carried away with my joy . . . because as we trotted round the corner of a hayfield that was nothing but stubble, I found myself flying off. I rolled as I was taught to; I had dressed warmly in layers, which was lucky. Most of me was protected from the stubble stalks of hay, most of me, except my face. Laughingly, I dabbed at the broken skin where the stalks had slipped in, grateful that I wouldn't have to explain my boxer-like injuries to my students. I had honestly looked like I lost a fight, and I had, only it was with gravity or the horse . . . or both! Either way, I got back on and finished the ride, knowing if it happened again, I would get up again.

Whether we are 10 years old, 21, 30, 50 or 80, we fall off horses. We keep falling off and we keep getting back on. Sometimes it's because someone else's comfort dumps us on the ground, where we learn humility for unkindness. Sometimes it's because we throw our weight right, when we should throw it left and we land on our face, causing more harm to vanity than the body for our lack of attentiveness. But whatever the reason, falling off horses makes us all better riders, if we let it.

Silver Screening

She knew she had to go; she didn't know why. She didn't even like
the cinema.

But...

The night before she had been tidying up from a client and her deck had
inexplicably scattered on the floor. Even more inexplicably, of the entire
deck, only three cards faced upwards. She was fortune teller enough not
to ignore so powerful a coincidence. So, to the cinema she went.

The smell of stale popcorn, the feel of aging velvet seats and
the clattering of the 'retro' film projector made her even more
uncomfortable than she already was. Not trusting her stomach, she went
straight past concessions and into a chair somewhere in the nondescript
middle. Checking her ticket again she still didn't know the film or what
it was about.

'The Last Game' seemed an unbearably ambiguous title; as the lights
dimmed and the screen flickered to life, Ana felt her mind wander. The
blacks and whites and grays seemed sharper than they should be for
an antique film. The frosted glass on the door in the opening shot read:
'Edge Agency, Private Investigations.'

A square-jawed, clean-shaven, broad-shouldered man in a suit came
out from behind the desk as the door was opened by a feminine
hand. "About time you got here," he ground out, "the board's been set
for an hour."

He indicated a Chesterfield chair next to a chessboard and the eyes of the camera looked down at the woman's hands as they leaned on the arms and lowered her into the seat. Ana squinted closely and the screen held still. *That bracelet . . . she's wearing my grandmother's bracelet!* she thought.

Ana looked down at her own hand to check the heirloom was still there; her eyes froze and broadened. Her skin, her clothes, were leached of all colour and she was gripping the arms of a Chesterfield chair. She looked back up at the screen to see the eyes of Mr. Edge, private detective, grinning, wolfishly at her.

Slowly, he reached for a pawn on the chessboard. "Let's play . . ."

Unexpected Door

Huh, it's . . . a door . . . just . . . a door, free standing, freshly painted, clearly labelled '221 B Lost Place'. Now I guess that might not have been so strange, except I could see it out my front window, in the middle of my vegetable garden.

Walking up to it I can't possibly say what made me reach for the lion-headed knocker, but you would, wouldn't you? Just to see what happened. Nothing. As it turns out nothing happened. I almost turned away at that point, really I meant to; I got as far as one step back the way I had come. Until a rosy glow shone from the bottom edge of my feet. *How odd,* I thought, considering the sun went down three hours ago.

I know it's impolite to enter without knocking, or since I already knocked, to enter without waiting to be invited. I can only think my lapse in manners was owing to some force beyond my control; I turned the doorknob. It opened easily, and silently, inward and I gaped at the interior. Well, I say the interior . . . if a landscape of lush paradisiacal meadows and forests off to a twilight-lit horizon can be considered an interior simply because I'm standing in a doorway. I stepped through because, well, you would, wouldn't you? No one was there to stop me, so it seemed as impolite not to enter as it had to open the door uninvited moments ago.

I'll assume it was the right and expected thing to do since the door closed behind me with a sound that suggested locking. Thinking I'd need to ask my host to let me out, I explored the grassy slope before me. Just inside the tree line stood a couple; beautiful, laughing delightedly and sharing in the sunshine and peace of this place. As they turned and saw me, grins spread across their face. "Staying for dinner?" the woman asked. When I nodded the man gestured toward a patch of lawn that looked more comfortable than any couch I've ever sat on.
I stared, and thought, and finally asked, "Mind if I stay?"
In unison the couple laughed and said they wouldn't have it any other way. As we walked off the woman handed me her basket of apples and said, "Welcome. I'm Eve, by the way."

Next Time ... Next Time

Their hands touch and their lips the same, his hand brushes her cheek. For a short time only, the lovers are together. But oh ... those times they are! At the end he whispers a swift goodbye and hands her a red rose. The kind he always gives when he must leave her. "Next time," he says, "will be longer, next time."

With an eager eye she waits for him, glancing out the window, trying to force the sun to set with her eyes. She sees lights but as she rushes to the door, she finds only the stars instead of headlights. These same stars they love to gaze at together, though now she curses them for tricking her. Finally, she hears footsteps and again the lovers meet. 'I am the only one he loves, his nights belong to me, coming faithfully to my arms, his actions speak volumes.' Her heart sighs in his embrace. Once again, he whispers "next time", and leaves her.

This time she knows there will be a next time. But what of the time after that, and the next time after that? There was a next time and a next. For months, he continued to say, "I love you, next time will be longer, sooner." She felt so sure his visits would come. *Next time, I will go to him. I will go before he is to come here, right at sunset shades, as they drift through the clouds.* She smiled and thought. *Yes, next time I'll go to him. Next time.*

She bought a dozen of the roses he usually gave to her and went to see her faithful lover. Carrying the glass vase, seeming light in her hands, topped full of her heart and love for him; she rang the doorbell. A light touch opens the door. A small child is standing there. From behind her, a woman's voice sounds, "Who is it darling?" and the owner of the voice appears. Followed by her husband. A sudden shock comes over our faithful lover. The husband is her faithful lover.

Let slip from her hands the glass vase shatters on the porch. Her heart crashes as the vase, splintering into a thousand splinters. The same with her hopes and dreams. *The shards,* she thinks, *one must have fallen on my chest for the pain there is insufferable!* Slowly the door shuts, and she knows there will be no next time. No more roses in the night, no more footsteps, no more headlights, only the cold tricking stars. "Who will come now, another to fool me, another to promise next time?" she asks those cruel stars.

Can I ever listen to the lovers' words passed silently in the night again, and know there will be a next time ... a next time that will last for always? Will I ever find one that I won't have to wait for? What will happen next time ... next time?

Ring Envy

This is a new one for me, a feeling, an impulse. To look every time
I see someone, for that symbol of unity. Not just in bars, when I see
someone I find attractive (to check if they are free to flirt with), but as a
casual glance on the train or in the elevator, standing in line for coffee
or shopping. I don't really know when it started, when I began longing
for what other people seem to have. I've had a ring; I've experienced
the happiness of that moment when eyes catch down that church aisle.
I've watched those I care about give and receive rings of their own, raise
families, build futures.

I was one of those little girls, with fairy-tale dreams, who knew what
kind of dress I wanted... what flowers, what colors, what music. I was
one of those little girls who dreamed of the kind of man I wanted
to sweep me away, of the happiness we would create for each other,
the unconditional love I would offer and hoped to receive. For me
this dream didn't last, not for lack of trying... from both of us... but
somehow it wasn't the dream I had hoped for. Now I keep trying to find
the next chapter, trying to turn the page in my fairy tale, still hoping
there is another chapter.

This symbol of union means many things to many people. To some it's
a signal of unavailability, a prior claim of belonging with someone else.
For some it's a preventative to feel safe; if it seems they are unavailable
they can justifiably turn down unwanted attention, regardless of its
reality. For some, greedy and malicious, it's a challenge... to have what
they can't, to take something that doesn't belong to them at someone
else's expense.

I can't pretend to know why someone would try to 'steal' someone who is already committed to another, to hurt someone they may never meet. I can tell you I find myself looking more and more frequently at the occupied ring fingers of those around me with envy.

When younger I feel like I never bothered to check at all, like youth was some kind of proof against claim. People did get married young; it's not like someone under 25 or even under 20 might not have already lost their heart. I feel like I have lost my heart many times, that should have had me looking at ring fingers as soon as I started hoping to acquire my own match. But somehow the wish to be claimed never brought to mind the idea I might be too late when I saw someone my age I liked.

Now, having found and lost a love I looked for once, I'm back on the search. Almost before I look at the rest of the person, I look at the ring finger. Even now as I muse on my commute from work, I can't decide if I look out of jealousy or so I don't get my hopes up. If I know before I'm attracted to a person that there is hope or none, maybe, just maybe I'll find someone new, to make me the envy of hopeless romantics like me . . . still hoping.

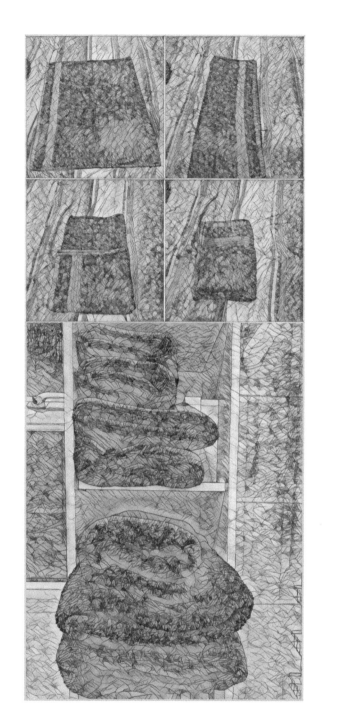

Folding Towels

The fresh laundry reminds me of home, of growing up helping Mom fold things warm and straight from the dryer. Especially towels. I know how strange that is, but one memory stands out. I was folding towels, fluffy and smelling like the detergent, when my mother stopped me putting one on the pile.

"No, hun, like this," and then she demonstrated:

- Corners together, fold on the long edge.
- Then again on the long edge, so it is quartered.
- Make sure the stripe is on the outside if there is only one.
- Then fold it in thirds along the short edge, again, keeping the stripe on the outside.
- In the cupboard the rounded edge faces out, not the flat edge side.

"Why does it matter?" I asked, not to be difficult, just to understand.

"Because that's the way my mother always did it, and she taught me to do it that way," my mother replied. As if that was the most logical reason and way to do anything there could possibly be.

And of course, it is.

Thirty or more years later, in another country, for all my life, I have folded my towels that way. It never occurred to me to find a faster or different way. It never occurred to me to try and save closet space by making them thinner, folded flatter.

It never occurred to me not to follow my mother's example, as she followed my grandmother's. Not just in folding towels, but in all things, all things I learned by her example. I try to follow in her footsteps. Her kindness and compassion always inspired me to be so to others. Her cooking recipes also inherited from my grandmothers, that we cooked together, are made every time I need a little comfort. Their scent fills the house and I am transported back home to the braided rugs, brickwork floor and wooden table of my mother's kitchen.

Like her compassion, like her cooking, like her towels . . . I am folded in the memories of my mother.

I am happy.

I Don't Want to Write About Lockdown (Part 2)

Despite what I say in verse four, there is no resisting it, no stopping the reflection on the paradigm shift in the world. I don't want to, but I have to. We all do. Deciding what parts of the 'new' world we want to keep, what parts need to go; what parts of the 'old' world we want to resurrect, what parts we need to excise (or exorcise as may be). I was lucky enough to be in a 'key worker' job, teaching, which meant my life was not as impacted as others. My day to day was more normal than most. Whether it was online or face to face — well PPE covered face — I was teaching ... doing too much work at too short notice with no time or help outside of the staff and admin at my school, my colleagues in the trenches. Everyone wanting answers and no one having them about lessons, technology, socialisation and exams. Somehow, like always, we got it done. Twice. I can only hope the new-found, long overdue, appreciation of parents for what exactly teachers do will last. Though I'm reasonably sure it won't.

I'm not what anyone would class as an introvert; I thrive in social situations. Not only do I thrive, I gain immense self-worth and self-esteem from gathering people together, creating communities in my home, feeding people and fostering friendship and conversation over huge meals. So, the loss of the ability to have people in my house for big meals and gatherings was great. Simultaneously, it was a relief. I do love hosting and making sure people I love are having a good time, but not being allowed to let me off the hook, out of the responsibility I enjoy so much. An enforced vacation that I still can't decide if I liked or benefitted from. Just like my job, my socialisation moved online exclusively in the beginning and mostly stayed that way even after things began to open up. I didn't miss the restaurants or the pubs, not in and of themselves, not the way everyone else seemed to. I've never felt so odd, so weird, so freakish as when I realised I wasn't suffering the loss of that kind of freedom everyone else seemed to be. Online contact, convenient and almost constant, was enough for me.

In fact, online contact expanded my life in ways I never could have predicted. First and foremost, connecting me more frequently with my family, 3,500 miles away. I can only afford to go home once a year, and I usually choose Christmas and New Year to enjoy the family traditions around that time. As bad luck would have it, I didn't go home during the holidays in 2019 because I was supposed to go for a family reunion in July of 2020 and my usual Christmas trip in 2020. Obviously neither of those things happened, which was more tragic than I can say. Two close family members passed around the time I was supposed to be there; I could do nothing but wish I had made it over to help and comfort. Despite this, being able to talk and share news regularly, is one of those habits I intend to keep. I feel closer and more connected to their lives than I have for years; I wish tragedy and emergency hadn't been necessary to realise how much I needed this.

Though tragedy had struck, there has also been triumph, and this online revolution had its role in that too. In May of 2020 I published my first collection of poetry, something I'd wanted to do for over 25 years. My dream had not included having to promote it exclusively online, but necessity is the mother of invention. I dove into the waters of social media and online events and discovered a web there to catch me, a network, of soulmates and fellow creatives I'd never have found otherwise. From one event to another, one link in the chain to the next. A changed world, a chain of connections, spreading further than anything else. I choose to focus on that, I choose to keep that as my enduring memory of the lockdown ... that which was found, NOT what was lost.

First Published in 'Life Inna Lockdown', 2020, Chapter 14

Acknowledgements

I'd like to thank my friends and family for their unwavering support and encouragement, and my test readers who helped me fight my own imposter syndrome.

I'd like to thank my students and colleagues who keep me honest and inspire me to keep challenging myself through my writing.
I'd like to thank the incredibly talented poets and artists from around the world who keep me inspired through online and live open mic nights.

I would especially like to thank: Raef Boylan and Ann Atkins who organize the Fire & Dust Poetry nights in association with *Here Comes Everyone* magazine, Dee Bailey and Simply Deez Events for her community zoom and network of inspiring people, the *Life Inna Lockdown* crew for their kindness and support.

Majority of this collection was written in a fabulous little bar in Wimbledon called Bertie's Bar. For the last several years this place has been a haven for my creativity with excellent staff, regular live music and a good group of regular drinking companions who put up with the eccentric poet. I want to thank all of them for making this and likely many more collections possible.

I'd like to thank the team at Conscious Dreams Publishing, Daniella Blechner, my Book Journey Mentor; Elise Abram, my editor and Oksana Kosovan, my typesetter and designer for continuing to give and support my voice in a beautiful way.

About the Author

Raised in the US but living permanently in the UK since 2003, Leah has an international point of view when it comes to the inspirational nature of the world around her. As a teacher of English Language and Literature for over ten years, and as a writer of poetry and fiction for more than 25, Leah has dedicated her life to the written word and its ability to inspire and connect people. To connect all of us to the world around us, our own thoughts and emotions and the experiences we all share as we travel the paths of our lives.

Leah holds degrees in English, Comparative Literature and International Studies from Pennsylvania State University in the United States as well as a Minor in German Language and Literature. At Canterbury Christ Church University Leah trained for a PGCE in teaching secondary English, Media Studies and Drama.

Most days are spent sharing her passion for the written word with young people, trying to comprehend British slang and making sure her coffee cup is never empty for the health and safety of others. She resides in Wimbledon, assisted in looking for inspiration by her cats Lord Merlin and Queen Mab.

Links to more about my work:
https://linktr.ee/LeahTheDreamer

Other Books by Leah Bailey

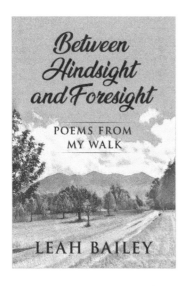

Between Hindsight and Foresight

In this collection you'll find poems that act as snapshots of a life, from teenage years through adulthood. They capture moments of joy, laughter, tears and trial. We all hope to find a way to express what we experience and feel, we all look for a way to feel less alone. Hopefully some can find that here.

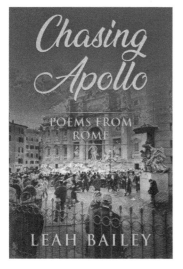

Chasing Apollo

Walk the streets of the eternal city with a modern traveler through ancient ruins. Each verse of Chasing Apollo is a step through, under and around the paths of Rome. In addition to the main poem, you'll find a number of stray poems inspired but the same trip in a unique kind of travel writing.

Spirit Of Fire & Dust

This anthology is an excellent representation of poems by attendees of Fire & Dust online events: an exciting mix of styles, voices and topics. Many regulars, headliners and newcomers — both in-person and Zoom — were invited to send in submissions.

Some poets went with the theme 'spirit of fire and dust', while others offered up pieces that reflect the body of work they've shared with us at previous gigs.

Life Outta Lockdown 2021: Beyond Closed Doors

This anthology is the sequel to Life Inna Lockdown 2020: Behind Closed doors. Members of an online community group record the living history of their lives during these trying times. Drawing from a wide range of ages and experiences for its authors, this book represents a unique perspective on the world as e go out into it once more

Conscious Dreams
PUBLISHING

Transforming diverse writers
into successful published authors

 www.consciousdreamspublishing.com

 authors@consciousdreamspublishing.com

Let's connect

Lightning Source UK Ltd.
Milton Keynes UK
UKHW020736280622
405026UK00006B/424

9 781915 522009